All About Mechanical Engineering

Don Herweck

Physical Science Readers:

All About Mechanical Engineering

Publishing Credits

Editorial Director
Dona Herweck Rice

Associate Editor
Joshua BishopRoby

Editor-in-Chief
Sharon Coan, M.S.Ed.

Creative Director
Lee Aucoin

Illustration Manager
Timothy J. Bradley

Publisher
Rachelle Cracchiolo, M.S.Ed.

Science Contributor
Sally Ride Science

Science Consultants
Jane Weir, MPhys

Teacher Created Materials
5301 Oceanus Drive
Huntington Beach, CA 92649-1030
http://www.tcmpub.com

ISBN 978-0-7439-0577-0

Printed by: 51497
Printed in: China

Table of Contents

Mechanical Playground

Think about being at an amusement park. Can you imagine the sounds and smells? Can you picture the rides—roller coasters, trains, spinning cups? An amusement park is a playground of **mechanics** (muh-KAN-iks) and motion.

Mechanics is a field of science that deals with motion and the causes of motion. **Engineering** (en-juh-NEER-ing) is the use of science and math to design, build, and run structures, machines, and **systems**. The basis of mechanics and engineering is found in Sir Isaac Newton's three laws of motion. Newton lived hundreds of years ago. His work has been key to many areas of science for centuries.

Amusement parks could not be built without the laws of mechanical engineering.

Newton's Laws

Newton's first law is about **force**. This law has two parts. First, it says that an object at rest will stay at rest if there is no outside force to put it into motion. Second, without outside force, a moving object continues in a straight line at the same speed forever. For example, if you kicked a ball and there was nothing to stop it, it would just keep going.

Newton's second law tells what happens to an object when force acts on it. When a force is applied, an object **accelerates** (ak-SEL-uh-reyts) or **decelerates** (dee-SEL-uh-reyts). That means it speeds up or slows down. So, if you push someone on a swing, the person and swing speed up. If the swinger drags his or her feet on the ground, the swing and person slow down.

The third law is about actions and reactions. It states that "to every action there is an equal and opposite reaction." This means that if a force is used, something will happen in response to that force to equal the energy of the force. For example, if you kick your feet backward while swimming, your body moves forward. You move forward with energy equal to the energy of the kick.

Newton's Laws of Motion

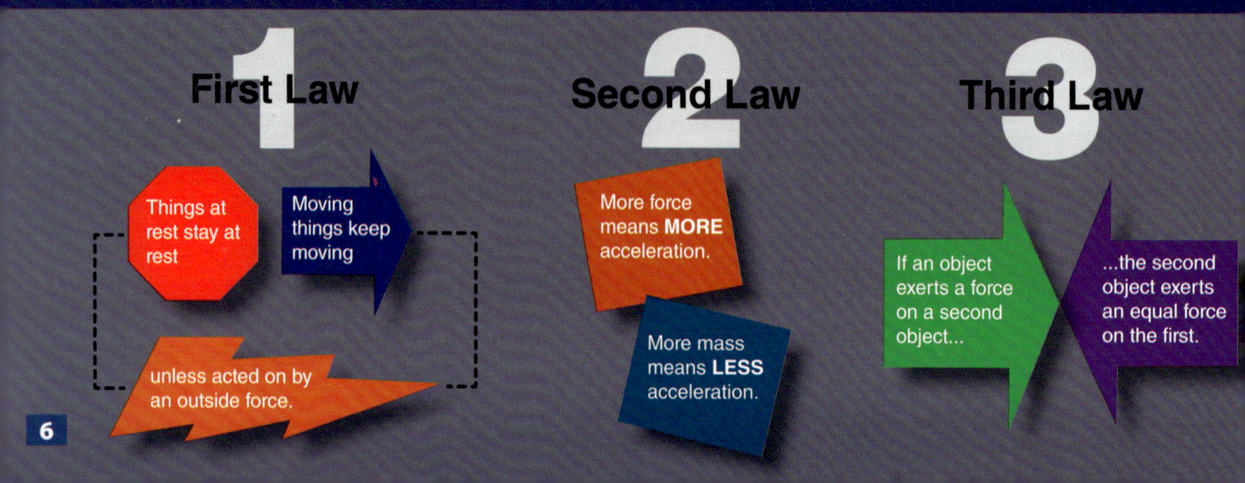

Free Fall

When you go to an amusement park, you probably don't think about the physics of force and motion. You can bet the people who built the park did. Free fall rides are a good example. They use the force made by motors to raise the vehicles and riders to the top. The amount of force needed varies based on the size and weight of the riders and cars. Once at the top, the real ride is based on the force of gravity. Down the riders go! They all drop at the same rate of speed. Then, the ride comes to a stop in gentle stages. If they stopped all at once at the bottom, they would be seriously injured. Newton's third law explains why.

Measurement

Mechanics is based on units of **measurement** (MEZH-er-muhnt). Engineers need to measure such things as length, time, and temperature. Each type of measurement is divided into equal parts. These parts are called units. A unit of length may be a centimeter or inch. A unit of time may be a second or a minute. A unit of temperature is a degree.

To design, build, or run anything, an engineer must first find exact measurements. That is why an engineer must be very good at math.

Dr. Waters works with length, weight, volume, and other units of measurement to design a boat that will stay afloat.

Oliver Smoot is big on measurement.

The "Smoot Unit"

In 1958, college students at MIT were ordered to measure the length of the Harvard Bridge in "Smoots." One Smoot was the height of their classmate, Oliver Smoot. The bridge measured as 364.4 Smoots long.

A Real "Ruler"

Did you know that some units date back to 6000 BCE? These units were often based on body parts. A good example of this comes from the 15th century. A yard was measured as the length between King Henry's nose and the thumb of his outstretched arm. The foot is based on the size of his boot.

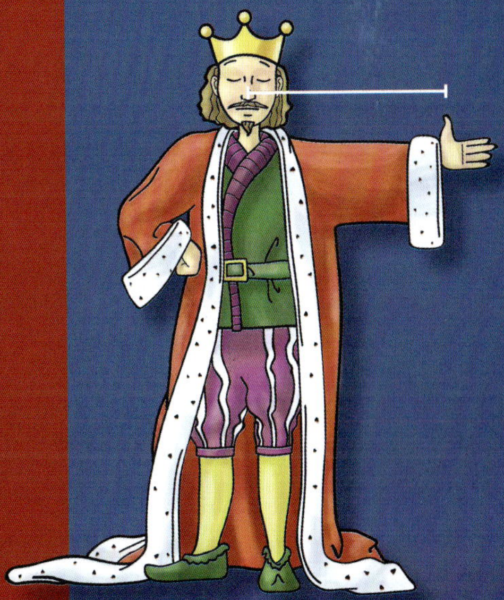

Dr. Jennifer Waters

Dr. Jennifer Waters is a naval architect. That means she plans, designs, builds, and runs boats of all kinds. To do this, she must first figure out the exact measurements for a planned boat. Dr. Waters works with length, weight, volume, and other units of measurement before a boat is finally ready to be used. She must also figure how much the boat can hold to stay afloat. And she must know the correct size and place for everything needed to make the boat go.

Motion

Mechanics and engineering also deal with **motion**. Motion is how, where, and why something moves.

In a Straight Line

The world and everything in it moves. Even mountains move as the earth turns. The world itself moves as it travels around the sun. From the tiniest atom to planets in space, everything is on the move.

Motion in a straight line is the simplest form of movement. If nothing gets in the way, there is no stopping, turning, or slowing down. It's just go, go, go from here to forever.

Distance, direction, and speed are some things that describe motion in a straight line.

A dolphin moves in three dimensions. It travels up and down, left and right, and backwards and forwards.

In Two and Three Dimensions

Dimensions are different ways things can be measured. Two dimensions are flat, like a drawing on a piece of paper. They are measured in length and height. Two dimensions are sometimes called 2-D. For example, a cannonball going through the air is in 2-D motion. It moves in a curved line that you could draw on a piece of paper. It doesn't move side to side.

Measuring in three dimensions uses length, height, and width. Think of a block of wood and how you would measure it. This is sometimes called 3-D. A helicopter moves in 3-D. It does not move in one fixed line. It can go up and down and turn from side to side.

Using mechanics, a scientist can figure out many things about the cannonball and the helicopter. Mechanics can help us know their locations, directions, and speeds.

Look Out Below!

David Smith, Sr., holds the world record for being a human cannonball. In 2002, he was fired from a cannon and traveled 61 meters (201 feet).

These game pieces have three dimensions. The game board shows two dimensions.

Velocity and Acceleration

Motion involves two important properties. They are **velocity** (vuh-LOS-uh-tee) and **acceleration** (ak-sel-uh-RAY-shuhn).

Velocity is the change in position over a set amount of time. It has both speed and direction. That means that velocity is not only how fast something is going, but also the direction in which it is moving. You have a certain velocity as you drive straight down the road in a car. If you go around a curve, your speed may stay the same. Your velocity does not though, because the direction has changed.

Acceleration is the change in velocity of an object. It is changing speed or direction. Acceleration is what you feel when the car starts moving from a stoplight. Negative acceleration, or **deceleration (dee-sel-uh-REY-shuhn),** is what you feel when a car is slowing down.

Many forces act on a cheetah leaping into the air after prey. The back legs force it up into the air as its velocity pushes it forward. Gravity forces it back down. At the exact moment the cheetah peaks in the air, it is balanced between the two forces.

For an object to move, force is needed. This involves a push or a pull. Force creates acceleration. The amount of acceleration depends on the mass of the object. **Mass** is the measure of how much matter the object is made of.

Objects in motion feel the effects from more than one force at a time. For example, a ball thrown into the air feels the force of the arm throwing it. Also, the ball feels the force of gravity when it is pulled back to Earth. The acceleration, velocity, and direction of the ball change because of the forces on it.

Can You Outrun the Laws of Physics?

Want to run faster? Use the laws of physics. Try this. Bend your arms and legs when running. That takes less force and energy. Lean forward and let the force of gravity pull you. Just remember to lean from your ankles and not your waist. To get the most out of leaning, place your foot down below or behind your center of gravity. Don't use your leg muscles to press down and back on the ground. It takes a lot of force to move your weight this way. Use your muscles to pick up your foot, and then let gravity do the work to lower it again.

Rotation

Another kind of motion in mechanics is **rotation**. Rotation happens when an object spins. A two-dimensional object rotates around a center point. If you spin a sheet of paper on a surface, the paper spins around a center of rotation. A three-dimensional object rotates around an **axis** (AK-sis). Imagine a spinning basketball. Picture a line going through the center of the ball. This axis is the center of rotation.

The finger shows where the axis of rotation is.

This Ferris wheel spins around an axis.

Basketball Court or Classroom?

A game of basketball uses many laws of physics. The spin you place on the ball causes a change in velocity. This makes the ball more likely to fall into the net. Physics is also needed to dribble. Your hand is the force that slaps the ball to the ground. The ground reacts to direct it up again. The rubber of the ball and the air inside it help with this. Physics even helps you catch a hard pass. Your hands and arms decrease the force of the ball, so you can catch it.

Dizzying Record

The record for the most continuous upright spins on one foot by an ice skater is 115. Lucinda Ruh accomplished this amazing feat.

Center of Mass

The **center of mass** is the point at which an object is balanced. For most people, their bodies' center of mass is right behind their belly buttons when they are standing straight. But, if they crouch or bend, the center of mass changes.

Have you ever seen a pregnant woman have a little trouble walking? That is because her center of mass is different from normal. She needs to find balance in a different way because of the growing baby inside her.

If you were to place a support under an object's center of mass, it can rest in balance. For example, when you sit on a chair, you are balanced on your bottom. This becomes your center of mass. If you were to sit on a board placed under the backside of your knees, you couldn't sit comfortably. The backside of your knees is not your center of mass.

Yoga positions, called asanas, require the body to hold its balance at the center of mass.

Snowboarding Physics

To make a perfect snowboard turn, you just need to remember the laws of physics. To stay up, you keep your body's center of mass over the board. To turn, you lean to the center of an imaginary circle. The amount you lean determines the angle of the snowboard. This angle unbalances the forces and determines the direction of the turn. When you lean, the force of gravity pulls you down the hill.

Surf's Up!

Have you ever watched a surfer and wondered how he or she stays upright? Well, the surfer is an expert in physics! A surfer must keep track of the center of mass of the surfboard and his or her body. Surfers must also know how the center of mass changes with each movement they make.

Engineers must understand the center of mass when building anything. There must be balance. Otherwise, the object can never do whatever it is supposed to do. It won't function, and it will probably collapse.

Look at the picture of the juggler. Notice the X on each object being juggled. The X represents the center of mass for each juggling pin. The juggler must understand the center of mass. That is the only way the juggler can toss and catch the pins. If the juggler doesn't understand the center of mass, he or she will miss or drop the pins.

The same is true for an engineer. Without understanding the center of mass, the engineer may make false measurements. There will be no balance. Whatever is being built may be unstable and collapse.

Center of mass keeps juggling pins and bridges in the air.

Fluid Mechanics

A **fluid** is a substance that can flow. Fluids take the shape of the container they are in. In physics, both liquids and gases are fluids. Scientists use **density** and **pressure** to describe fluids.

Density is a measure of how much stuff is packed into the space that the stuff occupies. Imagine a box of pillows. If you put in three pillows, the box might be full. However, you can cram more pillows in the box. The box with three pillows has a lower density than the box with more pillows.

Pressure is related to the force the fluid exerts on an object suspended in the fluid. A boat experiences pressure from water. A submerged boat feels the pressure from all sides.

Density and pressure affect one another. A submarine will be under more pressure if it is moving through a higher-density fluid, such as very cold water. A bowl of oil and water will separate with a layer of oil on top of the water. This is because the water has a higher density than the oil, and the pressure of the water pushes the oil up while the pressure of the oil keeps the water down.

Fluids add a new set of conditions to mechanics and engineering. Engineers must understand density and pressure as well as the rules of measurement, motion, and mass. This is especially important in the mechanics of designing boats.

In the late 1700s and early 1800s, an engineer named Robert Fulton worked with the properties of fluids to create new means of traveling by water. Today, engineers such as Dr. Jennifer Waters (page 9) continue this work.

The same mechanical laws apply whether a vessel is meant to stay afloat or submerge.

First Bottled Water?

The first vending machine was invented around 215 BCE. When a coin was dropped into a slot, its weight would pull a cork out of a spigot. Then, the machine dispensed a trickle of water. People couldn't have built this machine without the laws of fluid mechanics.

Engineering Through Time

Scientists have used mechanics and engineering from the earliest times to make life easier. On the next few pages are some of the major inventions in mechanics and engineering.

Early Engineering

Several simple machines were engineered long, long ago as tools. These tools assisted people with very common tasks. They are still in use today. Four such simple machines are the lever, the inclined plane, the wheel, and the pulley.

The first lever was probably just a large stick. It may have been used to move heavy things such as rocks. Imagine trying to lift a boulder. If you wedge a large board (lever) beneath it, you can move the boulder by pushing down on the lever.

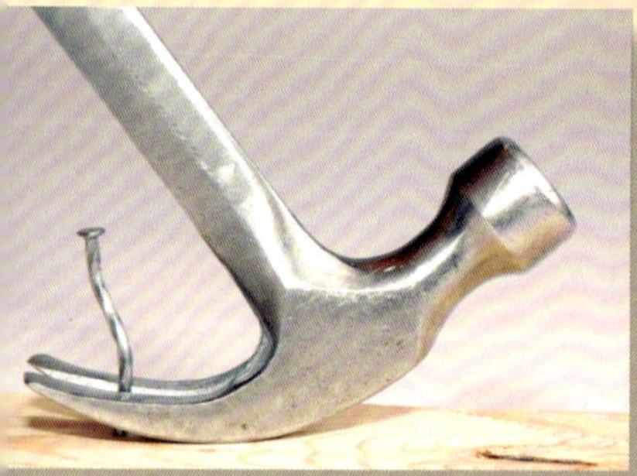

lever

Inclined planes were engineered to build roads and structures such as the pyramids in Egypt. An inclined plane works by lengthening the distance traveled to lift an object. Lifting a heavy box into a moving van can be difficult. But if you slide the box up a ramp (inclined plane), moving the box requires less force all at once.

The wheel allows easy movement of objects. A heavy object can be moved from one place to another by rolling rather than by lifting and carrying.

The pulley is a special wheel. It has a groove along the outer curve. A pulley has a rope that fits into the groove. Imagine tying one end of the rope to a bucket of rocks. Then pull the rope on the other side of the pulley. The pulley allows you to pull down rather than pull up. Sometimes pulling down is easier than pulling up.

Savery's "Miner's Friend"

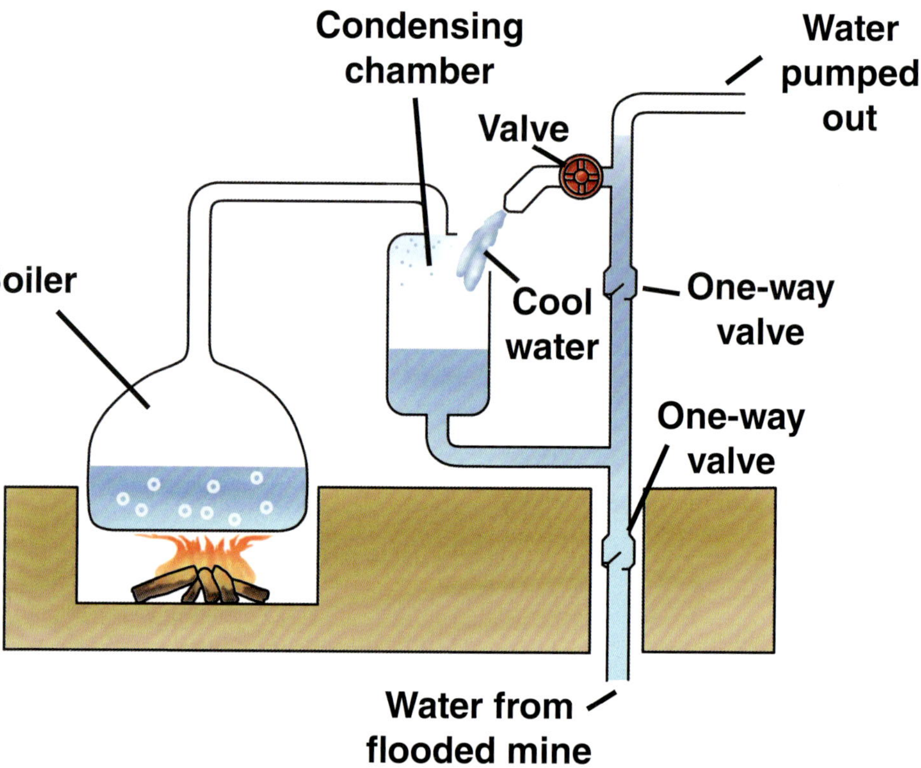

first steam engine

early motorcycle

early automobile

Modern Engineering

Many modern inventions were made possible through engineering. The first steam engine was created in 1698. It was used to pump water out of mines. Later, other engineers improved the design. This led to the invention of the modern steam engine. Robert Fulton applied the steam engine to boats to make them go. He created the first successful steamboat in 1807.

The first motorcycle was invented in 1885. An engineer put a gas engine into a bicycle frame. In the same year, another engineer put a new engine into the first practical automobile.

Flight was made possible by the engineering of the Wright brothers in 1903. Then, flight moved into space a few decades later. The work of many engineers led to modern rocketry.

When the water is boiled, steam pushes through into the condensing chamber. This forces water up and out of the tail pipe. Once the condensing chamber is full of steam, cool water is poured on it. The steam inside condenses into water, taking up less space, and pulling water up out of the mine below. Then the process is repeated, filling the chamber with more steam.

1903

Wright Brothers and an early airplane

1981

first space shuttle flight

2004

first private manned space flight, *SpaceShipOne*

Mechanics and engineering in the future will create things we can't imagine now. Many of today's inventions will see great improvements. Scientists expect breakthroughs in robotics (roh-BOT-iks), artificial (ahr-tuh-FISH-uhl) intelligence, and miniaturization (MIN-ee-uh-chuh-rye-zay-shun). That is the process to build things smaller and smaller.

Mechanics and engineering provide the rules. The rules let creative engineers make the things that advance and improve our lives.

Robotic devices will allow us to learn a great deal about space.

Virtual Physics

Are video games purely fantasy? Early versions were made without using the laws of physics. Today, virtual (VUR-choo-uhl) reality games use physics software to create an experience as close to real life as possible. Due to the power of newer game consoles as well as newer computers, games can be more lifelike than ever.

Objects in games are given mass by the programmers. So, a light object thrown against a heavy one will have less impact than items of equal weight. This special software makes a crashing vehicle behave more like a real vehicle. Even in the virtual world, the laws of physics apply.

Lab: Pressure, That Sinkin

Mechanical engineers must know all about the way things work in order to design, build, and run them. For example, a submarine engineer must figure out how to make a boat submerge or float. Without this information, the submarine will be useless.

Try this lab to learn something about floating and submerging. You will be on your way to becoming a mechanical engineer!

Materials

- a clear plastic bottle with a tight lid, such as a water bottle
- a squeeze condiment packet, such as for ketchup
- a glass
- water

Procedure

1 Fill a glass with water.

2 Place your unopened condiment pack into the water. The packet should just barely float. If it sinks, try another type of packet.

3 After you have a good packet, fill a clear plastic bottle with water.

Feeling!

4 Put your unopened condiment packet into the bottle.

5 Screw the top on the bottle.

6 The condiment packet is now a "boat." Squeeze the bottle to make your boat submerge, or go downward.

7 To make your boat rise, simply relax your hand.

What Is Happening?

The bottle filled with water has pressure in it. The condiment packet has a small pocket of air in it. When the bottle is squeezed, the air pocket in the condiment packet is made smaller. This is similar to adding water to the ballast tank of the diving boat or submarine. The increased pressure pushes the boat downward. The decrease in pressure brings it back up.

Glossary

acceleration—rate of change of velocity; speeding up or slowing down

axis—straight line around which an object rotates

center of mass—point in a body or system around which its weight is evenly balanced

deceleration—to reduce speed; to go more slowly

density—the amount of matter in a certain volume

dimension—a measurable extent, such as length, width, and heighth

engineering—putting scientific ideas to practical use

fluid—matter that has the ability to flow or be poured

force—a push or pull

mass—the amount of matter in any solid object or in any volume of liquid or gas

measurement—determination of dimensions

mechanics—branch of science that deals with motion and the action of forces on objects

motion—movement

pressure—the amount of force exerted by a fluid

properties—a special quality of something

rotation—the spinning of an object on its axis; turning

systems—a group of objects or units combined to form a whole and to move or work together

velocity—the rate of change of position

Index

Sally Ride Science

Sally Ride Science™ is an innovative content company dedicated to fueling young people's interests in science. Our publications and programs provide opportunities for students and teachers to explore the captivating world of science—from astrobiology to zoology. We bring science to life and show young people that science is creative, collaborative, fascinating, and fun.

Image Credits

Cover Shuttersttock; p.3 Photos.com; p.4 KB Studio/Shutterstock; p.4-5 Photos.com; p.5 (top) Photos.com; p.5 Photos.com; p.6 (top) Photos.com; p.6 Tim Bradley; p.7 Lisa C. McDonald/Shutterstock; p.8 (top) Public Domain; p.8 (bottom) Photos.com; p.8 (right) Courtesy of Jennifer Waters; p.8–9 Sandra Cunningham/Shutterstock; p.9 (left) Steve Liss//Time Life Pictures/Getty Images; p.9 (right) Tim Bradley; p.10 (top) Photos.com; p.10 (bottom) Sergey Popov/Shutterstock; p.11 (right) Denis Poroy/AP; p.11 (bottom) BrunoSINNAH/Shutterstock; p.12 (top) Photos.com; p.12 (top) Shutterstock; p.12 (first cheetah) Corel; p.12 (second Cheetah) Shutterstock; p12-13 (third Cheetah) shutterstock; p.13 (fourth Cheetah) Corel; p13. (Fifth Cheetah) Shutterstock; p12-13 (background) Shutterstock; p.14 (top) Photos.com; p.14 (left) Beth Van Trees/Shutterstock; p.14 (right) Dhannte/Shutterstock; p.15 Photos.com; p.15 (bottom) Phil Anthony/Shutterstock; p.16 (top) Photos.com; p.16 (bottom) Kristian/Shutterstock; p.17 Photos.com; p.18 Photos.com; p.18–19 Photos.com; p.19 (right) photos.com; p.20 (top) Danilo ducak/Shutterstock; p.21 Danilo ducak/Shutterstock; p.21 (right) Richard Seymour/Shutterstock; p.22 (top) Dan Briški/Shutterstock; p.22 (left) Jonathan Cook/iStockphoto; p.22–23 Tim Bradley; p.23 Library of Congress; p.24 (back) NASA; p.24 (front) Tim Bradley; p.24 (bottom left) Tim Bradley; p.24 (bottom center) Library of Congress; p.24 (bottom right) Library of Congress; p.25 (bottom left) The Granger Collection, New York; p.25 (bottom center) NASA; p.25 (bottom right) Courtesy of Derek Webber; p.26 NASA; p.27 D. Gifford/Photo Researchers, Inc.; p.28 (top) Danilo ducak/Shutterstock; p.28–29 Nicoll Nager Fuller; p.32 Getty Images